# MONTANA
*Portrait of a State*

# MONTANA

*Portrait of a State*

SALVATORE VASAPOLLI

GRAPHIC ARTS™ BOOKS

*To the gods of Olympoi. As they were in the heart and soul of Homer,
so they will always be in mine. To my aunts, Phyllis Marchese and Rose Pergola,
my uncle, Angelo Marchese, and my sister, Roseann Procopio, for their support.
To Stephen Jackson, curator of the Museum of the Rockies for all
his help. And to my loving mom, Angelina Vaspol.*
—Salvatore Vasapolli

Library of Congress Control Number: 2008927593
International Standard Book Number: 978-0-88240-753-1

Captions and book compilation © MMVIII by
Graphic Arts™ Books, an imprint of
Graphic Arts Center Publishing Company
P.O. Box 10306, Portland, Oregon 97296-0306
503/226-2402; www.gacpc.com

The five-dot logo is a registered trademark of
Graphic Arts Center Publishing Company.

President: Charles M. Hopkins
Associate Publisher: Douglas A. Pfeiffer
Editorial Staff: Timothy W. Frew, Kathy Howard, Jean Bond-Slaughter
Production Coordinator: Vicki Knapton
Cover Design: Vicki Knapton
Interior Design: Jean Andrews

Printed in the United States of America

FRONT COVER: ◖ On the east side of Glacier Park the clear
waters of Swiftcurrent Lake reflect the majesty of Grinnell Point.
BACK COVER: ◖ A limber pine marks the Pine Butte Swamp Preserve.
◀◀ An outstanding attraction on the Boulder River is Natural Bridge. Here
the river emerges from holes in the rock wall in a stunning 105-foot waterfall.
◀ Little Chief Mountain, left, and Dusty Star Mountain rise above St. Mary Lake,
one of the largest lakes in Glacier National Park. Glacier, designated a national
park in 1910, is arguably one of the most beautiful parks in the United States.
▶ Going-to-the-Sun—touted as the most scenic highway in the nation—
overlooks Logan Pass on the spine of the Continental Divide.
Fields of bear grass line the slopes nearby.

◄ The White Cliffs, here showing Sunrise Hole in the
Wall above the Missouri River, were described by Meriwether Lewis.
▲ A gallows frame (a hoisting head atop a mining shaft) stands sentinel above
a century of the mining past of Butte—once famous as the Richest Hill on Earth.
►► A storm develops near Square Butte in the Judith Basin. The area was named
by explorer William Clark to honor his lady friend in Virginia. Clark
and Judith Hancock were married following his return.

▲ In 1954, Montana dedicated Bannack as a state park.
The Methodist church, left, was built in 1877. Just one year after gold was
discovered at Grasshopper Creek, Bannack's population had grown to three thousand.
► Elkhorn's Fraternity Hall and the next-door Gilliam Hall date from the late 1800s,
when the mines reputedly produced some fourteen million dollars in silver.

▲ In Bannack, once the state's territorial capital, a young cowboy
pans for gold, and the look on his face says he has "struck pay dirt."
► Remarkably preserved by the dryness of the Montana climate, the
Graves House, left, rests beside the Methodist church in Bannack.
Established in 1863, Bannack was once the largest city
(population eight thousand) in Montana Territory.

◄ Bighorn Canyon, with Yellowtail Lake, is situated
in Bighorn Canyon National Recreation Area. This area has
been designated as a traditional Crow Tribal Vision Quest Site.
▲ Lured west by the Homestead Act of 1862 and the Great Northern
Railroad's promise of "a farmer's paradise," thousands sought Utopia,
attempting to extract a living from harsh, unyielding land.

15

▲ Boulders adorn 7,705-foot Northwest Peak, in the Percell Mountains. Known as the Purcell Mountains in British Columbia, the spelling changes to Percell as the range comes into Montana and Idaho.

▶ The upper Yaak Falls are a jewel situated in northwestern Montana's Kootenai National Forest. *Yaak* is an Indian word for "arrow."

◀ Construction of the Capitol Building in Helena began in
1899. Because of the state's rich history in copper mining, the Capitol
Rotunda is composed of copper. The building was opened for use on July 4, 1902.
▲ The statue in front of the Capitol depicts Civil War Union General
Thomas Francis Meagher, who served as temporary governor
of Montana in 1864 when the governor was away.

▲ The Cabinet Mountains were granted protection
within the National Wilderness System in 1964, the year the
U.S. Congress began the legislative process of providing
the ultimate protective designations to portions of the
country's wildest and most critical public lands.

▲ Deep winter arrives early, stays late, and,
through an ongoing process of freezing and thawing
that has continued for centuries, shapes the rocks of Ear
Mountain near the Bob Marshall Wilderness.

▲ Set off by quaking aspen, Little Chief Mountain, 9,541 feet high,
reveals the rock strata formations prevalent throughout Glacier Park.
► Makoshika State Park, in the rugged badlands of eastern Montana in
Glendive, is Montana's largest state park, encompassing some 11,400 acres.
►► The open spaces of the high plains of eastern Montana provide
ample territory for an abundance of prairie grasses and flowers.

◀ Glaciers in Glacier Park are few and receding.
Broken shards of slate are signs of Jackson Glacier's
passing. ∪-shaped, hanging valleys are also evidence of
glacier action that resulted in the park's astonishing geology.
▲ Snow pillows—pockets of air lifting snow ice into intriguing forms—
line the south shore of Lake McDonald, in Glacier National Park.

▲ These shield warriors, ancient images
painted on stone (pictographs), are still visible in
Bear Gulch Pictograph Canyon in the Big Snowy Mountains.
► Named for the Native people who once lived in the area, Kootenai
Falls boom through the cracked and colorful rocks of Kootenai
Gorge. The roar of these waters is heard long before
their cascading plumes can be seen.

◄ Storm clouds approach the Belly River Valley in Glacier
National Park. The park officially became part of the National Park
System on May 11, 1910, just twenty-one years following Montana's statehood.
▲ Winter provides the sublime conditions of deep powder and snow ghosts
for those skiing under the Big Sky. Here, John "Disco" Derby enjoys the
powder in backcountry access at Big Mountain Winter Resort.

▲ Ripple marks of red mudstone create the foreground for
paintbrush and the Garden Wall, whose jagged cliffs were formed by
glaciers cutting into the ridge. The Bishop's Cap crowns the wall on the left.
▶ Avalanche Creek tumbles from its beginning high in Avalanche Lake until
it reaches the Trail of the Cedars, becoming a small tranquil creek.

◄ Twilight reflects off Flathead Lake, a remnant of Lake Missoula, near
Rocky Point. Flathead is the largest freshwater lake west of the Mississippi.
▲ *Hook 'em cowboy!* Ed Jakubowski tries his luck in Lolo Creek's rapids.
►► A defiant capstone stands sentinel near Fort Peck Reservoir and
the Missouri Breaks. In 1805 when Lewis and Clark made their
way through this area, they found it to be a wildlife mecca.

▲ In a display of the power of water, tiny
Avalanche Creek, flowing from Avalanche Lake, cut
through massive rocks to create the gorge, whose rock walls
confine the creek as it tumbles toward the Trail of the Cedars.
▶ Rocks from the Garden Wall form a backdrop for
brilliant paintbrush, arnica, and rock vine.

◄ The Bridgers, like most of
Montana's mountains, are big-shouldered.
▲ Trophy bighorn sheep prepare to determine
dominance within the herd.

◄ The hand-carved grand stairway of the thirty-four-room Victorian
Copper King Mansion is lighted by stained-glass windows and ornate lamps.
In the 1880s, the mansion was the Butte home of mining industrialist W. A. Clark.
▲ Set off by the steep slate roof, the ornate facing of the attic windows of
the Copper King Mansion looks over uptown Butte. The three-
story mansion has been preserved as it was in the 1880s.

▲ The extraordinarily surefooted mountain goat
(*Oreamnos americanus*) flourishes in many of the state's still-wild
high places. The goats congregate in the lower valleys as winter arrives.
▶ A southern portion of the Chinese Wall, on the perimeter of the
Bob Marshall Wilderness—America's first designated Wilderness
Area—announces the eastern front of the Rocky Mountains.

▲ Aspen, trimmed in autumn's gold, frame 9,080-foot
Chief Mountain. Seventy million years ago the waters of a shallow
sea covered the entire Northern Rockies. For a hundred thousand centuries
an uplift has continued to raise this and the other mountains of the region.
▶ Glacier National Park's Mokowanis River flows over Gros Ventre Falls.

◄ In the Absaroka-Beartooth Wilderness, the 12,500-
foot-high Silver Run Peak rises above a small alpine lake, or tarn.
▲ The moving water beneath the winter cover of Lake McDonald creates ice
heaves near Apgar Village. Apgar Mountain rises in the distance.

▲ White-water rafters, next to House Rock on the Gallatin
River, enjoy one of the state's many great rides. The Gallatin offers
numerous rapids—House Rock, Mad Mile, and Bill's Rock, to name just a few.
► The bell-shaped flowers of the perennial harebell herald spring along the
Hyalite Reservoir near Palisade Falls in the Gallatin National Forest.
►► A snag on Lake Como rises before the Bitterroot Mountains
high in the wild country near the Montana-Idaho border.

◄ A pine tree, roots creeping around rock
outcroppings in the Dice Creek drainage, frames
Baldy Mountain in the Pioneer Range, which has been
proposed for Wilderness designation before the U.S. Congress.
▲ Balsam leaf flowers overlook Helena, seat of the state's government and
the site of early gold discoveries. The gold-producing creek, now covered
by the city's main street, is appropriately named Last Chance Gulch.

◄ Billion-year-old rocks can be
seen spanning Singleshot Mountain. The
St. Mary's River waters a golden carpet of aspen trees.
▲ "Flowers on the wing," painted ladies augment a small bouquet
of dandelions among the grasses of the forest floor. Also known
as the thistle butterfly and the cosmopolitan, the painted lady
may be the most widespread butterfly in the world.

▲ Flaming scoria rock greets the sunrise in the Yellowstone
River Valley. Scoria is formed by coal seam fires that bake the
surrounding material into a red, bricklike rock. Erosion resistant, scoria
is found capping soft clays that make up the badlands of eastern Montana.
▶ Prickly pear cactus blooms in the Charles M. Russell National Wildlife Refuge.
▶▶ Potholes, such as this one near Haystack Butte, dot the great prairie
empire bordering the west front of the Rockies.

◄ A setting sun throws shadows atop Sprague Creek Canyon
and glistens off the waters of Lake McDonald in Glacier National Park.
▲ Finding root in the shallow, rocky soil, whitebark pines are common in the
subalpine zones around six thousand feet above sea level. Their seed
cones provide nourishment for numerous species of wildlife,
ranging from birds and rodents to grizzly bears.

▲ The clear waters of Swiftcurrent
Lake on Glacier's east side hold a mirrorlike
reflection of 13,005-foot Mount Gould.

▲ The longest undammed stretch of water in the
Lower 48 states, the Yellowstone River struggles in winter's
grip. The Yellowstone begins as a mere trickle from Younts Peak
in the Teton Wilderness. Over the next 676 miles, it grows to
a powerful, turbulent river before it joins the Missouri.

▲ Among winter recreational opportunities available on 10,876-foot Sphinx Mountain are both cross-country and downhill skiing.

▶ A granite notch high on 10,157-foot Trapper Peak reveals the eroding mountains of the Selway-Bitterroot National Wilderness Area.

▶▶ Makoshika State Park encompasses capstones, towers, and mounds, and the fossil remains of such dinosaurs as tyrannosaurus rex and triceratops.

◄ The Humbug Spires Primitive Area, near Butte, has been
proposed for federal Wilderness designation. These massive outcroppings
of quartz monzonite present rock-climbing challenges for climbers of every ability.
▲ Aspen is perhaps the most widely distributed tree in the nation. This stand
is near the Red Rocks Lake National Wildlife Refuge. From 1898 to 1917
the Monida-Yellowstone Stage Line brought visitors to the area.

◀ Timberline Creek trickles into the
sunset-tinted waters of Lake Timberline, high
in the Absaroka-Beartooth National Wilderness Area.
▲ "The Prickly Pear is now in full blume," wrote Captain
Meriwether Lewis, "and forms one of the beauties
as well as the greatest pest of the plains."

▲ White lupines grace the Shields Valley,
with the Crazy Mountains on the horizon. The Shields
Valley nestles between the Bridger Mountains to the west, the Crazy
Mountains to the east, and the Absaroka Mountains to the south. One of
the state's prime trout streams, the Shields River meanders through the valley.
► Dead cedar bakes on the sunbathed rocks of the Pryor Mountain Wild Horse
Range, so named because some 120 wild horses range this wild land.

◄ A bighorn sheep ewe peers over a cliff in Gardiner Canyon.
The females give birth in the spring and lie in seclusion for a week prior to
rejoining the herd with their lambs. Ewes may weigh up to two hundred pounds.
▲ The Wild Horse Range of the Pryor Mountains forms a backdrop beyond the
colorful cliffs and slow-moving waters near Devil Canyon Overlook.

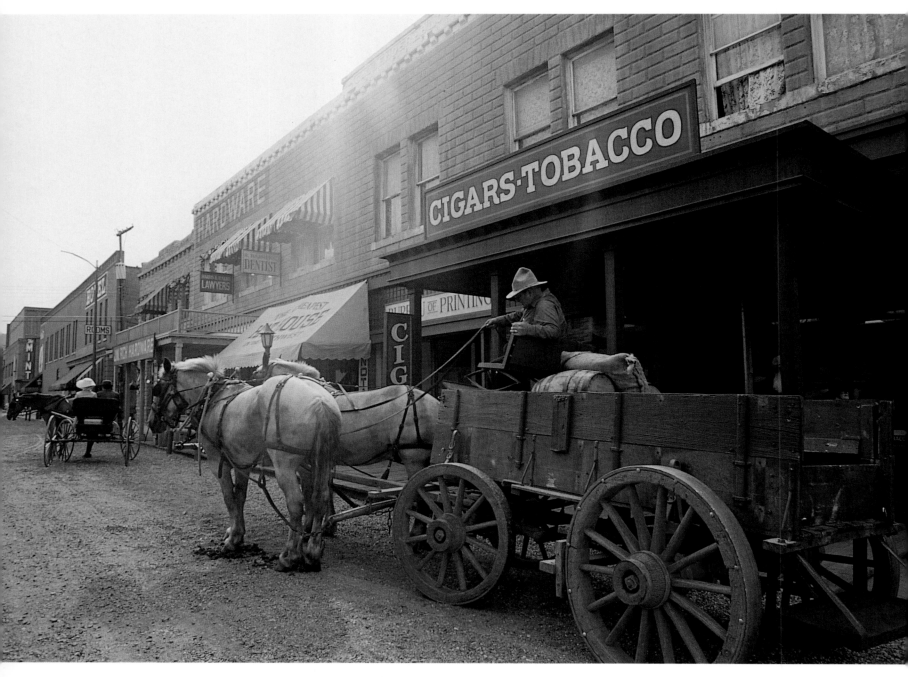

▲ The natural scenery and the towns of
Montana have been the backdrop for many movies,
including the award-winning *A River Runs Through It*, directed by
Robert Redford. The movie used this scene in Livingston.
▶ A frontier barber shop waits for customers in the
renovated Havre Beneath the Streets. The town
of Havre was founded in 1891.

◄ A native son celebrates North American Indian Days, an
annual event hosted by the Blackfeet Tribe. A four-day celebration held the
second week in July, it is one of the largest gatherings of U.S. and Canadian tribes.
▲ Native lodges—tepees—rise stark and black against the last light of
sunset. Because of their efficient design and their historical
significance, traditional tepees are still popular today.

81

▲ A long Montana twilight reveals cattails
silhouetted against pond waters in the Lee Metcalf
Wildlife Refuge. The refuge was established
in 1963 to protect habitats for migratory
birds and a variety of wildlife.

▲ As late winter brings the promise of
spring, snowbanks collapse into the upper
Gallatin River near Fan Creek. In other seasons,
the upper Gallatin is a popular site for fishing
for trout, rainbow and cutthroat.

▲ The state's world-class ski areas attract
thousands of skiers annually. The slopes offer every
class of skiing from beginner to extreme. Here, expert skier
Eric Knoff takes to the air on Bridger Bowl's infamous ridge.
► Big Horn Canyon, which surrounds the Yellowtail Reservoir, is
the setting for this winter canyon suite. Yellowtail Dam, at the
mouth of Bighorn Canyon, impounds flows of the
Bighorn River for multipurpose use.

◄ The Ross Creek Cedar Grove Scenic Area protects trees that
range up to 175 feet tall, with trunks that may reach eight feet around.
▲ From its beginning with the first house in 1883, Great Falls continues as
a center that serves agriculture, America's military defense, and transportation.
Lewis and Clark arrived at the Great Falls of the Missouri River on June 13,
1805. It took them seven days to portage around the falls.

▲ A miniature alpine daisy, finely attuned
to its wild environment, clings in delicate
balance with the tumbling waters of Palisade Falls.
► The grace and beauty of nature's infinite shapes are
evident in rocks in the lapping waters of Bell Creek
in the Lewis and Clark National Forest.

◄ This boulder lies near the confluence of Bear Creek
and the Middle Fork of the Flathead River in northwest Montana.
▲ The rising sun backlights cattails at the Lee Metcalf Wildlife Refuge.
►► A double rainbow encircles Golf Course and Rifle Range, near
Yellowstone's Black Canyon and Rattlesnake Butte.

▲ In 1911 cowboy artist Charlie Russell was commissioned
by the state to paint a large mural to be mounted in the new House of
Representatives wing of the capitol. The result was the monumental 25-by-
12-foot canvas, *Lewis and Clark Meeting the Flatheads in Ross's Hole.*
▶ The impressions of early artists can still be seen in these deer
figures in Pictograph Caves located near Billings.

◄ Autumn's gold flanks the Gallatin River, named by Lewis and
Clark on July 27, 1805, in honor of Secretary of the Interior Albert Gallatin.
▲ Wood, rock, and sky complement the Absaroka Mountains along Upper Mission
Creek Road in the Gallatin National Forest. The forest is part of the one-third
of Montana that is held for the public under national ownership.

▲ Cold temperatures combine with the current of the Missouri to
create standing ice in Canyon Ferry Reservoir near Helena, the state's capital.
▶ A kayaker rides the white water of the Gallatin River. Camping, rafting, and
fishing are only a few of the recreational opportunities offered along the river.
▶▶ Dried, twisted, and decaying roots and the broken rock of a limestone
outcropping set off the snowy Beartooth Mountains in the background.

◀ Sandstone formations provide the pedestal for a national
landmark, Capitol Rock, in the Custer National Forest. Capitol Rock is so named
because the massive white limestone uplift resembles the nation's Capitol Building.
▲ The Crow Indians still know these lands as home. Red Rock Canyon is located in Crow
Country, with Red Pryor Mountain and the Pryors beyond. The Pryors were named for
Nathaniel Pryor of the Lewis and Clark Expedition. Starting from the badlands to
the south, the mountains rise five thousand feet in just twenty miles.

▲ The Paradise Valley, north of Yellowstone Park, is home to some
of the state's earliest ranch families as well as many of our newest arrivals.
▶ The trapping and binding of sediments by minute organisms formed this
stromatolite boulder beneath Glacier Park's ancient Garden Wall.

◄ Sedge along the Missouri River is not only beautiful; it also
provides food for deer and elk. More than one hundred species of the
flowers are found scattered throughout the Rocky Mountains and high plains.
▲ A lone cabin nestles in the trees near the snowbanked Gallatin River.

▲ Clouds over the Absaroka Mountains
portend thunder and rain, which will soon join sky
and land as one. The Absaroka-Beartooth Wilderness Area
provides habitat for large predators, such as grizzlies and wolves.
▶ Lake McDonald, in Glacier National Park, was formed when
a 2,000-foot-high glacier gouged out the 472-foot
depression about twenty thousand years ago.

◄ North of the town of Jordan,
the eroded hillsides form the Reid Coulee.
▲ The breaks near the Tongue River provide contrast to waters
that begin in Wyoming, finally joining the Yellowstone River at Miles City.
►► High benches, forests, valleys, and rocks add to the variety
of scenery in the Tongue River Breaks.